Baby Animals

Illustrated by Tien

Platt & Munk, Publishers/New York

From the day they are born, puppies have
a keen sense of smell.

Designed by Craigwood Phillips, A Good Thing, Inc.

The baby koala bear lives high in the trees and rides on its mother's back.

Lion cubs like to wrestle and fight over food their mother brings home from the hunt.

Baby goats like to sneak up behind each other and butt with hard little foreheads that soon will grow horns.

Just like children, kittens have toys
and play games.

The baby kangaroo is called a "joey." It rides in a pouch on its mother's stomach.

Once baby bunnies have opened their eyes, their mother needn't watch over them as closely as she did when they were first born and helpless.

The baby lamb looks like a soft and wooly toy. It spends its first few months close to its mother's side.

A calf is frisky and strong from the day it is born.

Bear cubs are born in caves during winter. When they go outside in spring, their mother has her paws full feeding them and keeping them out of mischief.

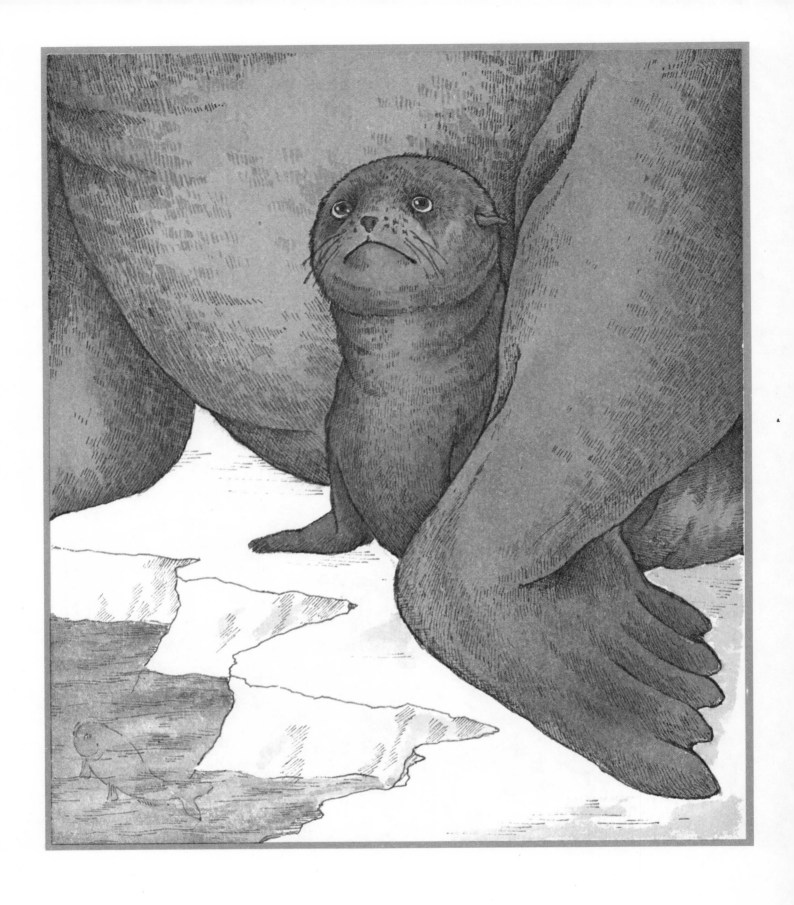

Baby seals are called "pups." When a pup is old enough, its mother dumps it in the sea, and it must learn to swim in a hurry.

Piglets are born eight to ten at a time.
They have neat, round bodies with soft
silky hair and small curly tails.

A baby elephant has flappy ears and a long trunk just like its parents. It will take 25 years to become fully grown.

Fuzzy yellow ducklings follow their mother in a line and seldom stray.

The baby chimp hangs onto its mother's fur while she swings through the trees.

On bitterly cold days, the baby penguin snuggles in the warm space between its parents' feet.